Mmm...
I am going to
eat you!

Canolfan Peniarth would like to thank the School of Early Childhood and the School of Initial Teacher Education and Training for their help in preparing the books in this series.

© Text: Angela Rees, 2011
© Images: University of Wales Trinity Saint David, 2011

Published in 2011 by Canolfan Peniarth.

University of Wales Trinity Saint David asserts its moral right under the Copyright, Designs and Patents Act, 1988 to be identified respectively as author and illustrator of this work.

Sponsored by the Welsh Government.

1

2

3

5

9

13

Glossary

wasp

gwenynen feirch
picwnen

butterfly

glöyn byw
pili–pala
iâr fach yr haf

bird

aderyn

fly

cleren
pryf

ladybird
buwch goch gota

spider
corryn
pry copyn

spider web
gwe pry cop
gwe corryn

moth
gwyfyn

bumblebee
cacynen

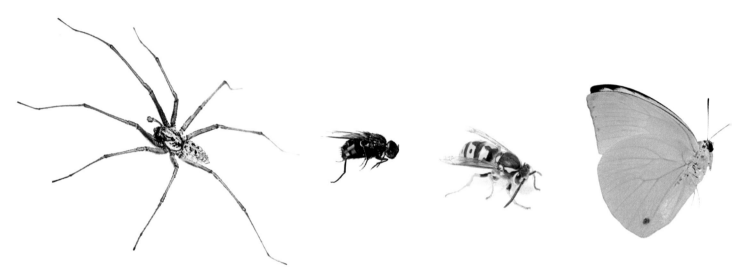